Bad Girl Gone Good

12 Ways to Renew Your Identity

The Workbook

Shirley P. Auguste

High Bridge Books
Houston

Contents

Introduction

The purpose of this workbook is to help those seeking to find the good in themselves through discovering who God created them to be. Everyone has the ability to be good enough to be used by God. The question is, "Do you believe you are good enough?"

When I first wrote the book, *Bad Girl Gone Good*, I wasn't sure what to expect or even if others would want to read the book. All I wanted to do was share how God had been good to me and how He kept me through some of my hardest days.

I wanted the world to know that if God could turn my heart and life around, He could definitely do it for anybody else if they truly desired. I was hoping others would see that God could use anyone for His purposes.

I wanted the world to know that God is not this complicated or harsh God that some people make Him out to be. I wanted people to know that God is not harsh or cruel but loving and forgiving. Yes, He would allow people to suffer the consequences of their sins, but everything will have either a good or negative consequence. It's not God that is cruel; it is our actions or the actions of others that may cause a negative consequence. Regardless of the negative consequences, God can use and turn anything into a positive message.

If you are seeking and really want to see what God can do, get a pen, open your heart and mind, and let's begin this journey.

Directions

This is a self-paced workbook. It is best if you attempt to work on this daily to begin developing a habit of meditation and prayer. Life does happen and can get busy, and you have to learn to make time for yourself. If you don't make time for yourself, who will?

Start by taking fifteen (15) or thirty (30) minutes a day to do a question/page and read the scripture. Once you are in the habit of taking time for yourself, then you can begin to schedule times longer than thirty (30) minutes a day.

When you are answering the questions, be honest with yourself and know that this is a journey between you and God. This is a process of self-evaluation and healing. You have to remove the negatives within to begin filling with positives. As long as there are negative thoughts or feelings, it will be hard to receive anything positive. Don't hold anything in; let it all out. Don't worry about grammar or spelling. Let yourself go and be completely honest.

When you finish the workbook, you should be able to go back and see a difference of how you used to think. However, there is no guarantee because this is **your** journey, and the growth will depend on your willingness to let go and begin a new way of thinking and believing.

A prayer to begin each session

"God, I come asking that you remove any and all barriers that would keep me from growing into the person you want me to be. Help me to be open to receive and hear. Help me to remove self and allow the Holy Spirit to reign within. I come before you with a humble and willing heart. Thank you, Father, for what you have done, are doing, and will do. I worship and give you praise. Amen."

What are your thoughts of a "bad boy or bad girl?"

_____

_____

_____

_____

_____

_____

Do you see yourself as a bad boy/girl? Explain your thoughts.

_____

_____

_____

_____

_____

_____

How do you see yourself? (For example, "I see myself as a good person that helps others because…" or "I see myself as a horrible person because…"

_____

_____

_____

_____

_____

_____

_____

_____

_____

_____

_____

Do you believe it is possible for people to change? Why or Why not?

_____

_____

_____

_____

_____

_____

What are you hoping to gain or learn from reading the book and completing the workbook?

_____

_____

_____

_____

_____

_____

What are some things you believe might be a barrier(s) in completing the book or workbook?

_____

_____

_____

_____

_____

_____

_____

Let's pray and bind up any and all of the barriers…

> *"Truly I say to you, whatever you bind on earth shall have been bound in heaven; and whatever you loose on earth shall have been loosed in heaven. Again I say to you, that if two of you agree on earth about anything that they may ask, it shall be done for them by My Father who is in heaven. For where two or three have gathered together in My name, I am there in their midst." (Matthew 18:18-20)*

In the name of our Lord and Savior, Jesus Christ, I bind up _____ (*say the things you wrote*) and claim victory over them. I stand on your Word and believe that with the Holy Spirit, I can and will overcome all of those barriers. They will not have any strongholds in my life. My mind and heart are open to receive and begin the process of transforming my life. In the Name of Jesus, Amen.

What myths do you believe about Christians?

_____

_____

_____

_____

_____

_____

How did you come to believe some of those myths?

_____

_____

_____

_____

_____

_____

Being a Christian simply means that the person is a follower of Christ and trying to live a life of morals and values. No Christian is perfect or ever will be. Christians are regular people who have turned their lives around and are trying to live according to the gospel of Jesus Christ. Yes, there are some who model the life much better than others. Yes, there are some who make others want to run from the church or anything pertaining to Jesus Christ or God because of their attitudes, behaviors, or way of life. However, one or two people do not represent any one religion or group of people. We have to stop generalizing and stereotyping. Everyone is an individual and will make a mistake of some sort.

The idea that a Christian is supposed to be perfect or have it all together is a myth. When Jesus picked His disciples, He was looking for willing hearts. Do you have a willing heart? Jesus said to his disciples,

> *"Follow Me, and I will make you fishers of men." (Matthew 4:19)*

And everyone dropped everything and went with Jesus. Yes, things are different today in many ways and God would not want you to do anything irrational. It all starts with a willing heart and open ears to hear. I can't say what God is or isn't going to do with your life. However, I can say that God has a great sense of humor and will use you in positive ways that you would never imagine. No, things aren't going to be easy or without any issues. If anyone tries to tell you that it is supposed to be easy, I would be very cautious to listening to that person.

As you begin this new journey, things and people around you will change because you are changing. Remember to remain humble and understand that everybody may not understand. Do not judge or condemn anyone because everyone goes on their journey at different times or differently. It is a Christian's responsibility to at least plant a positive seed and become a light.

How many real and heartfelt friendships (people you can call on at any time, pray with, ask for help or advice, and will listen to despite how hard the message is that they have to give to you) do you have? How do you know they are real friends and not surface friends?

_____

_____

_____

_____

_____

_____

_____

_____

_____

_____

_____

Are you being true-blue or being an imitator of the world? Evaluate what kind of friend you are to others. Are you honest about your likes, dislikes, and feelings? Or do you simply conform to be accepted and keep certain people around?

_____

_____

_____

_____

_____

_____

Chapter 1

The Beginning of a Journey

How did you feel after reading the poem, "The One"?

_____

_____

_____

_____

_____

_____

Did you know your mind is a battlefield? What are you doing to protect your mind?

_____

_____

_____

_____

_____

_____

What are you battling in your mind?

_____

_____

_____

_____

_____

_____

As you begin to answer this question, be careful not to blame another person. People cannot keep you from being happy, having peace, or experiencing joy because we can only control ourselves. You may want to control a person or make him or her feel a certain way, but you can't. Remember, you can ONLY control yourself.

Is there anything keeping you from experiencing true happiness, love, peace, or joy? Are you trying to force anyone to love you when they have already expressed that they do not love you?

_____

_____

_____

_____

_____

_____

_____

_____

_____

_____

"For you were called to freedom, brethren; only do not turn your freedom into an opportunity for the flesh, but through love serve one another. For the whole Law is fulfilled in one word, in the statement, "You shall love your neighbor as yourself." But if you bite and devour one another, take care that you are not consumed by one another. But I say, walk by the Spirit, and you will not carry out the desire of the flesh. For the flesh sets its desire against the Spirit, and the Spirit against the flesh; for these are in opposition to one another, so that you may not do the things that you please. But if you are led by the Spirit, you are not under the Law. Now the deeds of the flesh are evident, which are: immorality, impurity, sensuality, idolatry, sorcery, enmities, strife, jealousy, outbursts of anger, disputes, dissensions, factions, envying, drunkenness, carousing, and things like these, of which I forewarn you, just as I have forewarned you, that those who practice such things will not inherit the kingdom of God. But the fruit of the Spirit is love, joy, peace, patience, kindness, goodness, faithfulness, gentleness, self-control; against such things there is no law. Now those who belong to Christ Jesus have crucified the flesh with its passions and desires. If we live by the Spirit, let us also walk by the Spirit. Let us not become boastful, challenging one another, envying one another." (Galatians 5:13-25)

Have you faced yourself? What are some things you would like to see improved in your character, attitude, or life?

_____

_____

_____

_____

_____

_____

_____

Are you at a crossroad in your life, a time when some significant decisions need to be made? Have you prayed about them? Explain.

_____

_____

_____

_____

_____

_____

_____

_____

_____

_____

_____

Are you getting ready to make a decision based on hurt or pain? What decisions have you been struggling to make that involve pain or hurt? Whatever you do, never make any decisions based on pain or hurt.

_____

_____

_____

_____

_____

_____

"If indeed you have heard Him and have been taught in Him, just as truth is in Jesus, that, in reference to your former manner of life, you lay aside the old self, which is being corrupted in accordance with the lusts of deceit, and that you be renewed in the spirit of your mind, and put on the new self, which in the likeness of God has been created in righteousness and holiness of the truth. Therefore, laying aside falsehood, SPEAK TRUTH EACH ONE of you WITH HIS NEIGHBOR, for we are members of one another. BE ANGRY, AND yet DO NOT SIN; do not let the sun go down on your anger, and do not give the devil an opportunity. He who steals must steal no longer; but rather he must labor, performing with his own hands what is good, so that he will have something to share with one who has need. Let no unwholesome word proceed from your mouth, but only such a word as is good for edification according to the need of the moment, so that it will give grace to those who hear. Do not grieve the Holy Spirit of God, by whom you were sealed for the day of redemption. Let all bitterness and wrath and anger and clamor and slander be put away from you, along with all malice. Be kind to one another, tenderhearted, forgiving each other, just as God in Christ also has forgiven you." (Ephesians 4:21-32)

Chapter 2

How We See Our World

What are some ways you see the world? Do you believe you are correct? Explain.

_____

_____

_____

_____

_____

_____

What are some false beliefs that people have about other people or about life in general?

_____

_____

_____

_____

_____

_____

_____

Which of those false beliefs do you have in your life?

_____

_____

_____

_____

_____

_____

_____

Sometimes we face so many issues or experienced a variety of traumas in lives that we try to hide behind alcohol, drugs, sex, fancy clothes, or expensive material items. As a result, we never really deal with our issues. Take a step toward dealing with your issues. Don't let hurts, pains, or any sort of life trauma keep you from experiencing complete peace.

Facing hurts and traumas can be difficult and may require seeking out professional Christian counseling. I can tell you first-hand that you won't regret it. When I first saw a Christian counselor, I was concerned about all of the negative perceptions and asked the counselor, "Am I crazy?" The counselor looked at me and stated, "No, you are not. It is the people that don't go to counseling that usually end up crazy." I chuckled and felt relieved. We talked about people seeing a doctor to care for their physical body, dentist for their teeth, and a mechanic to fix their car. However, people rarely see the importance of seeing a counselor to care for their mind.

Our minds have to deal with so much more than our bodies, yet we often neglect it. Don't be one of the ones that neglect your mind. Be whole, and make sure you are healthy physically, mentally, and spiritually. Do a self-evaluation.

What are you running from? Stop running and be determined to face and deal with all of your hurts, grudges, and issues that have bound you mentally and emotionally.

_____

_____

_____

_____

_____

_____

Chapter 3

The Pain

Dealing with pain is never easy, and people usually try to run from dealing with it. Running from pain never solves the problem. Instead it usually manifests itself in different ways.

Think back on some of the issues that caused you pain. No matter how silly or ridiculous you think it may be, if it is a source of pain for you, write it down.

_____

_____

_____

_____

_____

_____

_____

_____

_____

_____

_____

_____

What event has caused you to change? Either good or bad.

_____

_____

_____

_____

_____

_____

As a young child, I made a lot of vows that affected me as I became older. I had to think about the vows and deal with them. I realized some of the vows were made during moments of anger. Unfortunately, those vows became a part of me, and I made some poor decisions based on vows I never broke. It is important to realize those childhood vows and break them. It is unfortunate, but we have a lot of grown people acting as middle or high school kids because they never dealt with youth issues and never learned how to handle things properly as adults.

What vows did you make as a child that still haunt you?

_____

_____

_____

_____

_____

_____

Are you aware of those vows, or did you choose to block them out to avoid dealing with the pain?

_____

_____

_____

_____

_____

_____

_____

As we grow into adulthood, there are things we must change in our lives. How many times have you seen a grown person act worse than a teenager? Most likely, more than you would like. It is unfortunate but common. Age really is a mere number. Maturity is the ability to deal with conflict, difference of opinion, and with managing one's affairs responsibly. A person's character, attitude, and how they deal with life issues determine if they are acting as a mature adult.

As I observe people, I can see the difference in an "adult" and a "child-like adult." This is not an insult or meant in a derogatory way. It is meant to shed light on why people are not perfect or may act irrational at times. These observations have helped me to evaluate my own behavior.

The first step is always recognizing the issue. The second is making the decision to deal with the issue and be different.

> *"When I was a child, I used to speak like a child, think like a child, reason like a child; when I became a man, I did away with childish things." (1 Corinthians 13:11)*

Have you realized how special you are? Take a few minutes to write down some things about yourself (hair, looks, size, talents, things you like, and anything positive you can think of). What are some good things people have said about you?

_____

_____

_____

_____

_____

_____

_____

_____

Do you know your worth? Explain.

_____

_____

_____

_____

_____

When you look in the mirror, are you happy with whom you see? Explain.

_____

_____

_____

_____

What are you going to do to make sure you have inner peace and joy every time you look at the person in the mirror?

_____

_____

_____

_____

_____

If you were not aware that God created you uniquely, read Psalms 139:13-18. You were created to do great things. God knows you are not perfect and wants you to grow in His Word and into the person He wants you to be.

"For You formed my inward parts; You wove me in my mother's womb. I will give thanks to You, for I am fearfully and wonderfully made; Wonderful are Your works, And my soul knows it very well. My frame was not hidden from You, When I was made in secret, And skillfully wrought in the depths of the earth; Your eyes have seen my unformed substance; And in Your book were all written. The days that were ordained for me, When as yet there was not one of them. How precious also are Your thoughts to me, O God! How vast is the sum of them! If I should count them, they would outnumber the sand. When I awake, I am still with You." (Psalms 139: 13-18)

Chapter 4

The Growing Pain

As you read, how do you feel? Can you relate?

_____

_____

_____

_____

_____

_____

What destructive words are you accepting from others?

_____

_____

_____

_____

_____

_____

_____

Why do you keep listening to destructive words? What is it in your past that keeps you holding on to the destructive words?

_____

_____

_____

_____

_____

What pain is deeply rooted in you?

_____

_____

_____

_____

_____

_____

_____

What regrets are you holding on to?

_____

_____

_____

_____

_____

What loss has caused you to stop living fully?

_____

_____

_____

_____

_____

_____

_____

What are you running from?

_____

_____

_____

_____

_____

_____

Are you spinning out of control?

_____

_____

_____

_____

_____

_____

_____

If someone is always against you, why do you keep going back around them or begging for their attention?

_____

_____

_____

_____

_____

_____

As you realize the things you are running from and causing you pain, it is important for you to know that God can take anything and use it for good. Don't let the negatives keep you down or cause you to feel as if there is no hope. There is always hope with God on your side.

"Many are the plans in the mind of man, but it is the purpose of the Lord that will stand." (Proverbs 19:21, ESV)

"And we know that for those who love God all things work together for good, for those are called according to his purpose." (Romans 8:28, ESV)

"For I know the plans I have for you, declares the Lord, plans for welfare and not for evil, to give you a future and hope." (Jeremiah 29:11, ESV)

"But Jesus looked at them and said, "With man this is impossible, but with God all things are possible." (Matthew 19:26, ESV)

Chapter 5

Lost and Searching for Hope

As you evolve and begin removing the negatives from your life, it is important to find positive role models or an accountability partner. You are never too old to have a role model. Look at the people around you or who have accomplished the things you want to accomplish. You have to know where you want to go to achieve the things you want to achieve in life.

It is definitely good to have an accountability partner. This is a person that will be open and honest with you, and with whom you can be the same with them. This person will hold you accountable on the things you want to improve in (i.e. spiritually, professionally, etc.). You have to be careful when selecting an accountability partner because this is a long-term commitment and requires that both parties are willing to be open and transparent. Most of all, everything stated is only between the two of you and no judgment is allowed. You have to be able to give and receive critical comments for improvement to each other. This person must be someone of the same gender.

Do you have a mother or father figure trying to help you? Have you shown them gratitude?

_____

_____

_____

_____

_____

_____

_____

Who were the people that helped guide your steps?

_____

_____

_____

_____

_____

Have you recognized and shown your appreciation for those in your life who helped you accomplished your goals? Think of some ways you can show your appreciation.

_____

_____

_____

_____

_____

_____

_____

Will you give back by being a parental figure to help a child or by helping a young adult succeed? What are some ways you can help another?

_____

_____

_____

_____

_____

_____

Now that you are taking a closer look at your life, it's time to evaluate a couple of areas. Some things may seem redundant, but it's about looking deeper and evaluating.

Do you have real friends? How do you know that they are real and not simply surface friends (people that only hang out or share your joys because they believe they may gain something from you)?

_____

_____

_____

_____

_____

_____

What is keeping you from making a bad choice?

_____

_____

_____

_____

_____

_____

Are you making the same choices as the people around you?

_____

_____

_____

_____

_____

_____

To be unique, you have to be willing to do the things that you enjoy doing. You don't have to do what everyone else is doing just because they feel it is "normal." What is "normal" is doing something positive that you enjoy doing, even if no one else wants to do it.

Who or what has caused you to make a vow of not feeling emotions?

_____

_____

_____

_____

_____

_____

_____

What parts can you relate to in the book? Why do you believe you can relate to it?

_____

_____

_____

_____

_____

Take a few minutes to meditate on the poem, "Feeling Alone and Wondering When." Have you ever felt as if you have waited for an eternity for something you desired?

_____

_____

_____

_____

_____

_____

_____

Have you ever felt as if you were running and searching for God? Explain. How did it make you feel?

_____

_____

_____

_____

_____

What are some things that have kept you from improving your life? Why are you letting it hold you back?

_____

_____

_____

_____

_____

_____

_____

_____

Who are some of the people that bring out the worst in you? What are you doing to keep from losing yourself around that person or those people?

_____

_____

_____

_____

_____

What are you doing to help improve that relationship? What have you decided about that relationship?

_____

_____

_____

_____

Chapter 6

The End Is Near

Have you ever felt as if all hope is lost? When and why?

_____

_____

_____

_____

_____

_____

Have you ever been in a situation when you knew the end was near and there was no salvaging? What were the clues? What made you realize there was no hope?

_____

_____

_____

_____

_____

_____

_____

Have you vented about the things in your life that brought you down?

_____

_____

_____

_____

_____

_____

What keeps you in bondage and from being free to worship and live the way God intended for you?

_____

_____

_____

_____

_____

_____

_____

_____

What mess are you in, and why are you refusing to recognize that it is a mess?

_____

_____

_____

_____

_____

_____

To remove the mess, you have to recognize it and move forward. You can't move forward if you are going to continuously look back. It is time that you put the things of the past in the past and begin to move forward. Acknowledge and release!

What are your demons?

_____

_____

_____

_____

_____

Are you willing to face them to become the person God created you to be? What do you believe God wants you to accomplish or become?

_____

_____

_____

_____

_____

_____

When you begin to make changes in your life and deal with past hurts, be careful who you confide in or talk to. Make sure the people you confide in are positive, non-judgmental, and willing to keep your information private. If the person is always telling you about other people, they might be telling your business to others. Ask God for wisdom in everything you do.

Are you listening to counsel from people who do not know the whole story? Think about the people you are talking to. Do they know the details, and can they provide wise counsel?

_____

_____

_____

_____

_____

_____

Who is influencing your family that should not be? Sometimes we trust and find out later that certain people should not have been given the opportunity to provide counsel to us and our loved ones. You live and learn.

_____

_____

_____

_____

_____

_____

_____

Is your life yours or one to be dictated by others? Basically, are you making decisions for your life based upon dreams, desires, and things you've prayed about, or are you making decisions to please other people? Write a couple of decisions you've made and evaluate them.

_____

_____

_____

_____

_____

_____

The wonderful thing about life is waking up to another day! When you wake up, you have another opportunity to get right what went wrong the day before. If you hurt someone, hopefully you realized it on the same day. If not, don't delay and try to make right all the things that you did wrong the day before. Life is too short to be too proud to apologize or hold a grudge.

Take a few minutes and think about some things you would like to improve. Don't let pride, ego, or anger hold you back from making peace or letting go of an issue that brought pain.

_____

_____

_____

_____

_____

_____

Have you grown up mentally to recognize that grown-ups make decisions that help improve their life and mental state? What are some decisions you need to make to improve your life and mental state? Think about your relationships, career, finances, and spirituality.

_____

_____

_____

_____

_____

_____

_____

_____

_____

_____

_____

_____

What is the breaking point that will help you draw closer to God? What are some things stopping you from drawing closer to God?

_____

_____

_____

_____

_____

What lie are you living? Sometimes we form a life around a lie to impress others or to make ourselves feel good. In reality, it is a disaster waiting to explode. Facing self and the lie that has been in place can be difficult. Don't be afraid to face it.

_____

_____

_____

_____

_____

_____

Are you ready to accept the truth to begin healing and repairing your life and mental state? Explain why you are ready.

_____

_____

_____

_____

_____

_____

God has been waiting for you! Don't believe the lies about God from the world. He is after your heart. If you are ready, it isn't that hard and won't be painful.

To begin the journey with Christ…

Step 1 – Recognize that you are a sinner (everyone is).

"Therefore do not let sin reign in your mortal body so that you obey its lusts, and do not go on presenting the members of your body to sin as instruments of unrighteousness; but present yourselves to God as those alive from the dead, and your members as instruments of righteousness to God. For sin shall not be master over you, for you are not under law but under grace." (Romans 6:12-14)

Step 2 – Ask God to forgive you for your sins.

"What then? Shall we sin because we are not under law but under grace? May it never be! Do you not know that when you present yourselves to someone as slaves for obedience, you are slaves of the one whom you obey, either of sin resulting in death, or of obedience resulting in righteousness? But thanks be to God that though you were slaves of sin, you became obedient from the heart to that form of teaching to which you were committed, and having been freed from sin, you became slaves of righteousness. I am speaking in human terms because of the weakness of your flesh. For just as you presented your members as slaves to impurity and to lawlessness, resulting in further lawlessness, so now present your members as slaves to righteousness, resulting in sanctification." (Romans 6:15-19)

You may say a prayer from your heart or say this one: "Lord, please forgive me of my sins. Help me to know you better and to walk away from things that used to keep me bound in sin."

Step 3 – Say the prayer of salvation.

> *"That if you confess with your mouth Jesus as Lord, and believe in your heart that God raised Him from the dead, you will be saved; for with the heart a person believes, resulting in righteousness, and with the mouth he confesses, resulting in salvation. For the Scripture says, 'WHOEVER BELIEVES IN HIM WILL NOT BE DISAPPOINTED.' For there is no distinction between Jew and Greek; for the same Lord is Lord of all, abounding in riches for all who call on Him; for 'WHOEVER WILL CALL ON THE NAME OF THE LORD WILL BE SAVED.'" (Romans 10:9-13)*

Congratulations!!! Today is your new spiritual birthday! When someone asked if you are saved, you may answer, "Yes, I am saved because I professed Jesus Christ and accepted Him into my heart." Write today's date:

My spiritual birthday: _____

Now, the real work begins, and I will be the first to say, put on the Armor of God daily because things are NOT always going to be easy. Remember, you have just made Satan and his demons angry because you are no longer following wrong ways.

> *"Finally, be strong in the Lord and in the strength of His might. Put on the full armor of God, so that you will be able to stand firm against the schemes of the devil. For our struggle is not against flesh and blood, but against the rulers, against the powers, against the world forces of this darkness, against the spiritual forces of wickedness in the heavenly places. Therefore, take up the full armor of God, so that you will be able to resist in the evil day, and having done everything, to stand firm. Stand firm therefore, having girded your loins with truth, and having put on the breastplate of righteousness, and having shod your feet with the preparation of the gospel of peace; in addition to all, taking up the shield of faith with which you will be able to extinguish all the flaming arrows of the evil one. And take the helmet of salvation, and the sword of the Spirit, which is the word of God. With all prayer and petition pray at all times in the Spirit, and with this in view, be on the alert with all perseverance and petition for all the saints, and pray on my behalf, that utterance may be given to me in the opening of my mouth, to make known with boldness the mystery of the gospel, for which I am an*

ambassador in chains; that in proclaiming it I may speak boldly, as I ought to speak."
(Ephesians 6:10-20)

Step 4 – Get a book of devotions to help you begin a habit of prayer and meditation daily.

You can purchase one at a Christian bookstore or at almost any bookstore. If you go to a Christian bookstore, they should be able to help you find one. Be sure to pick up a study Bible so you may read as you are doing your devotions.

Step 5 – Find a Bible-believing church.

As you are looking and visiting different Bible-believing churches, pray and ask God to help you find the right church for you. Remember, no church is going to be perfect, and all churches will have people that are going to misrepresent Him at times. You are not going to church to judge or find the hypocrites. You are going to church to hear the Word of God to help improve your life. Most of all, you have to learn to build relationships with people in the church.

Step 6 – Try to stay out of places that are going to cause you to fall back into a habit or situation that caused you to sin.

Step 7 – Write down the excitement and how you feel, so you will always be able to remember the joy that entered your heart when you made this decision.

_____

_____

_____

_____

_____

_____

_____

_____

_____

_____

_____

_____

_____

As you enter into chapter seven, you are going to go deeper. Be ready to explore and remove as much hidden baggage as possible. Don't give the devil anything to use against you. Admit and deal with self and any other issue that might be a hindrance in your growth. Take a deep breath and proceed.

Chapter 7

God Does Miracles in the Midst of Chaos

Are you doing anything that is keeping you from experiencing peace and happiness?

_____

_____

_____

_____

_____

_____

Who is influencing you? Think about the people that are influencing you positively or negatively in your home, life, job, extra-curricular activities, or ministry.

_____

_____

_____

_____

_____

_____

What is brewing in your life that is going to cause a major change? Think about some good or bad things that are stirring and haven't been dealt with appropriately.

_____

_____

_____

_____

_____

Have you recognized how some of your selfish ways are negatively affecting those you care about? What are some examples of how selfishness can affect others negatively?

_____

_____

_____

_____

_____

_____

Are you in a selfish mindset or one that takes into consideration those who mean so much to you?

_____

_____

_____

_____

_____

_____

_____

_____

What are your priorities?

_____

_____

_____

_____

_____

_____

Will you listen to God to help a friend by putting your selfish needs and desires to the side?

_____

_____

_____

_____

_____

Are there people in your life that you really care about, those for whom you would be willing to stand in the gap?

_____

_____

_____

_____

_____

_____

_____

_____

_____

_____

_____

Who around you is hurting and may possibly feel alone?

_____

_____

_____

_____

_____

_____

Have you taken the time to reach out, or are you always expecting others to reach out to you?

_____

_____

_____

_____

_____

_____

When you reach out to people, is it for selfish reasons, or is it because you genuinely care and want to be a glimmer of hope?

_____

_____

_____

_____

_____

_____

Whose glimmer of hope will you be?

_____

_____

_____

_____

_____

_____

Before you begin to say, "I don't have the time," or "Other people are not my problem," read and meditate on Matthew 5:13-16:

> *"You are the salt of the earth; but if the salt has become tasteless, how can it be made salty again? It is no longer good for anything, except to be thrown out and trampled under foot by men. You are the light of the world. A city set on a hill cannot be hidden; nor does anyone light a lamp and put it under a basket, but on the lampstand, and it gives light to all who are in the house. Let your light shine before men in such a way that they may see your good works, and glorify your Father who is in heaven."* (Matthew 5:13-16)

What is your trigger?

_____

_____

_____

_____

_____

_____

Are you passing judgment on others who seem less fortunate than you or are going through a hard time?

_____

_____

_____

_____

_____

_____

Do you think you are that much better than others? Never be arrogant in thinking that you are a much better Christian or person than anyone else. Always remember that you don't know a person unless you have lived their life. What are some things that make you think you are better or worse off than others?

_____

_____

_____

_____

_____

What relationships are you forming or trying to improve? Why do you believe the relationship(s) need to be improved?

_____

_____

_____

_____

_____

_____

Do you have a growing relationship with God?

_____

_____

_____

_____

_____

Chapter 8

A New Beginning

You have been doing a lot of meditating and self-evaluation. You have begun your new journey. How much you have learned? How are you feeling?

_____

_____

_____

_____

_____

_____

Did you find yourself in the book? Where have you been able to make some connections with the experiences described in the book?

_____

_____

_____

_____

_____

_____

_____

Do you understand that everything you do impacts someone else? Name an example of when you knew you had influenced someone, and you could see the results (good or bad).

_____

_____

_____

_____

_____

_____

What sort of influence are you being on others? What sort of influence do you want to be?

_____

_____

_____

_____

_____

_____

_____

The Bible says to be an example for others:

> *"Prescribe and teach these things. Let no one look down on your youthfulness, but rather in speech, conduct, love, faith and purity, show yourself an example of those who believe." (1 Timothy 4:11-12)*

> *"Now accept the one who is weak in faith, but not for the purpose of passing judgment on his opinions." (Romans 14:1)*

> *"But you, why do you judge your brother? Or you again, why do you regard your brother with contempt? For we will all stand before the judgment seat of God. For it is written, 'AS I LIVE, SAYS THE LORD, EVERY KNEE SHALL BOW TO ME, AND EVERY TONGUE SHALL GIVE PRAISE TO GOD.' So then each one of us will give an account of himself to God. Therefore let us not judge one another anymore, but rather determine this—not to put an obstacle or a stumbling block in a brother's way." (Romans 14:10-13)*

Are there any emotions that are destroying you?

_____

_____

_____

_____

_____

_____

What emotions are controlling your life?

_____

_____

_____

_____

_____

_____

Do you view God as faithful? Explain.

_____

_____

_____

_____

_____

_____

God is very faithful and loves you. Do you believe God loves you?

_____

_____

_____

_____

_____

_____

"For the word of the LORD is upright, and all His work is done in faithfulness." (Psalms 33:4)

"Your loving kindness, O LORD, extends to the heavens, Your faithfulness reaches to the skies." (Psalms 36:5)

"The LORD'S lovingkindnesses indeed never cease, for His compassions never fail. They are new every morning; Great is Your faithfulness." (Lamentation 3:22-23)

Are you letting false prophets keep you from experiencing the peace of God?

_____

_____

_____

_____

_____

What are you doing to help yourself move forward from things that have caused you great pain?

_____

_____

_____

_____

_____

_____

_____

Always remember that everyone's journey is going to be different. NO ONE person will go on the exact same journey. Some people may have similarities in their journey, but the details will be different.

What has captured your mind?

_____

_____

_____

_____

_____

_____

What are you searching for?

_____

_____

_____

_____

_____

_____

What state of mind are you in?

_____

_____

_____

_____

_____

_____

What pain is life throwing your way?

_____

_____

_____

_____

_____

_____

What is keeping you from being able to progress?

_____

_____

_____

_____

_____

_____

_____

_____

_____

_____

_____

_____

Are you calling on God to help guide your steps and put the "self" away? Write a prayer that you believe you need to help in areas of weakness. Be sure to be specific and call them by name.

_____

_____

_____

_____

_____

_____

What are your thoughts on the statistics?

_____

_____

_____

_____

_____

_____

What are you doing to help build relationships? Are you encouraging others to stay together or to seek a healthy relationship?

_____

_____

_____

_____

_____

_____

What choices have you made that have caused damage to families, young girls and/or boys, women, or other men? (Examples could be simply not using positive words when talking about someone's spouse, or saying, "Everyone does it.")

_____

_____

_____

_____

_____

_____

What do you believe is the definition of a "good man" or a "good woman"?

_____

_____

_____

_____

_____

_____

There is a false belief that once a person accepts Jesus Christ, they will not have any obstacles, struggles, or temptations to deal with or face. Unfortunately, those beliefs are lies. You are still a human being and have begun working on your spirituality, which will eventually be apparent in your physical walk of life.

God did not swap out your spirit for a new one. You are simply beginning a process of transformation. Transformation is a process of being transformed. It is not easy, and there are times when you will have setbacks. However, God is a merciful and gracious Father. If and when you fall, don't just repent. Be sure you are sincerely and truly repenting from the heart. Someone who repents and justifies their actions isn't really a person that has repented from their heart.

It doesn't matter what others think, see, or believe about you. What really matters is what God is seeing in your heart. Always remember, you may be able to fool people, but you are never fooling God.

As you answer this question, be honest and prepared to face the things that you struggle with in your heart, mind, body, or in ways other people do not realize. What are you battling?

_____

_____

_____

_____

_____

_____

(This question is for singles) Have you spoken to God about where and what He wants you to do prior to getting into a relationship?

_____

_____

_____

_____

_____

(This is for non-singles) What are some things God has shown you that you need to improve in your relationship?

_____

_____

_____

_____

_____

Have you cast out the demons within yourself? Demons can keep you from moving forward in your walk with God.

_____

_____

_____

_____

_____

_____

(Singles) Are you really ready to be in a relationship?

_____

_____

_____

_____

_____

_____

(Non-Singles) Why did you get into your relationship? Are you letting people or obstacles in your relationship that should not be in it? What are ways you could improve the relationship and make sure God is the foundation of your relationship?

_____

_____

_____

_____

_____

Have you finished discovering who you are and what you like?

_____

_____

_____

_____

_____

It is time to let go of past dating relationships that are either keeping you from getting into a healthy God-founded relationship or are destroying your current relationship. Think about how your past relationships are or have affected your current relationships.

Do you have a belief about being friends with an ex-boyfriend or ex-girlfriend? How do you feel about your mate or future mate having a close bond with an ex?

_____

_____

_____

_____

_____

_____

How many spiritual husbands or wives do you have? _____

Do you want the little or big sex? Think and meditate on what you really want in a future or current relationship.

_____

_____

_____

_____

_____

_____

_____

Are you free from spiritual attachments?

_____

_____

_____

_____

_____

Are you having sex just to fulfill the flesh or to build your relationship with your spouse?

_____

_____

_____

_____

_____

_____

_____

What are you doing to protect your relationship?

_____

_____

_____

_____

_____

_____

Are you a home-wrecker? Do you know a home-wrecker? Have you been involved in destroying a relationship or marriage?

_____

_____

_____

_____

_____

_____

_____

What are your morals and values? If you don't have any, it is important to articulate and know what you believe and stand for morally.

_____

_____

_____

_____

_____

_____

Do you put emphasis on trying to help relationships work, or do you tear them apart?

_____

_____

_____

_____

_____

_____

_____

Chapter 9

The Healing

Healing is a step toward happiness and peace. Healing comes in different forms and looks different for everyone. Don't put a cap on how long or how your healing will take place. Once you had accepted Jesus Christ as your Lord and Savior, He began a new and wonderful work in you. Remember, you have been dealing with some issues for a long time, and it may take some time to overcome those issues. Again, do not put a timeframe on how long it should take. Imagine an onion or lettuce, and imagine peeling one layer away at a time. God is going to peel away everything that is keeping you from being whole and at peace.

"Therefore if you have been raised up with Christ, keep seeking the things above, where Christ is, seated at the right hand of God. Set your mind on the things above, not on the things that are on earth. For you have died and your life is hidden with Christ in God. When Christ, who is our life, is revealed, then you also will be revealed with Him in glory. Therefore consider the members of your earthly body as dead to immorality, impurity, passion, evil desire, and greed, which amounts to idolatry. For it is because of these things that the wrath of God will come upon the sons of disobedience, and in them you also once walked, when you were living in them. But now you also, put them all aside: anger, wrath, malice, slander, and abusive speech from your mouth. Do not lie to one another, since you laid aside the old self with its evil practices, and have put on the new self who is being renewed to a true knowledge according to the image of the One who created him—a renewal in which there is no distinction between Greek and Jew, circumcised and uncircumcised, barbarian, Scythian, slave and freeman, but Christ is all, and in all." (Colossians 3: 1-11)

What are you doing to heal? Think about some things you are doing besides reading and doing this workbook.

_____

_____

_____

_____

_____

_____

Are you living a false life, or are you being true to yourself?

_____

_____

_____

_____

_____

_____

Are you really applying your beliefs in your everyday life? Write your beliefs down and evaluate the areas in your life that have changed.

_____

_____

_____

_____

_____

_____

Will others be able to see that you are saying and doing what you have said you would do? What will others say about your walk? Will they be able to see a difference?

_____

_____

_____

_____

_____

_____

_____

What kind of influence are you being on others? If you are not sure, write the kind of influence you would like to be.

_____

_____

_____

_____

_____

_____

_____

Chapter 10

Beginning of Change

You have been walking and praying for a change, and God heard your prayers. No matter the struggles or challenges, keep on being faithful in your walk. You are becoming much stronger than you could have ever imagined.

How did you use to handle different challenges, and how you are able to handle them now?

_____

_____

_____

_____

_____

_____

"Now I say this, brethren, that flesh and blood cannot inherit the kingdom of God; nor does the perishable inherit the imperishable. Behold, I tell you a mystery; we will not all

sleep, but we will all be changed, in a moment, in the twinkling of an eye, at the last trumpet; for the trumpet will sound, and the dead will be raised imperishable, and we will be changed. For this perishable must put on the imperishable, and this mortal must put on immortality. But when this perishable will have put on the imperishable, and this mortal will have put on immortality, then will come about the saying that is written, 'DEATH IS SWALLOWED UP in victory. O DEATH, WHERE IS YOUR VICTORY? O DEATH, WHERE IS YOUR STING?' The sting of death is sin, and the power of sin is the law; but thanks be to God, who gives us the victory through our Lord Jesus Christ. Therefore, my beloved brethren, be steadfast, immovable, always abounding in the work of the Lord, knowing that your toil is not in vain in the Lord." (1 Corinthians 15:50-58)

What are you trusting God to do in your life?

_____

_____

_____

_____

_____

_____

"Sing for joy in the LORD, O you righteous ones; Praise is becoming to the upright. Give thanks to the LORD with the lyre; Sing praises to Him with a harp of ten strings. Sing to Him a new song; Play skillfully with a shout of joy. For the word of the LORD is upright, And all His work is done in faithfulness. He loves righteousness and justice; The earth is full of the loving kindness of the LORD. By the word of the LORD the

heavens were made, And by the breath of His mouth all their host. He gathers the waters of the sea together as a heap; He lays up the deeps in storehouses. Let all the earth fear the LORD*; Let all the inhabitants of the world stand in awe of Him. For He spoke, and it was done; He commanded, and it stood fast. The* LORD *nullifies the counsel of the nations; He frustrates the plans of the peoples. The counsel of the* LORD *stands forever, The plans of His heart from generation to generation. Blessed is the nation whose God is the* LORD*, The people whom He has chosen for His own inheritance. The* LORD *looks from heaven; He sees all the sons of men; From His dwelling place He looks out On all the inhabitants of the earth, He who fashions the hearts of them all, He who understands all their works. The king is not saved by a mighty army; A warrior is not delivered by great strength. A horse is a false hope for victory; Nor does it deliver anyone by its great strength. Behold, the eye of the* LORD *is on those who fear Him, On those who hope for His loving kindness, To deliver their soul from death And to keep them alive in famine. Our soul waits for the* LORD*; He is our help and our shield. For our heart rejoices in Him, Because we trust in His holy name. Let Your loving kindness, O* LORD*, be upon us, According as we have hoped in You."* (Psalms 33)

How are you growing and demonstrating your faith in God?

_____

_____

_____

_____

_____

_____

_____

_____

_____

_____

_____

Chapter 11

Change Taking Place

"Nevertheless knowing that a man is not justified by the works of the Law but through faith in Christ Jesus, even we have believed in Christ Jesus, so that we may be justified by faith in Christ and not by the works of the Law; since by the works of the Law no flesh will be justified. But if, while seeking to be justified in Christ, we ourselves have also been found sinners, is Christ then a minister of sin? May it never be! For if I rebuild what I have once destroyed, I prove myself to be a transgressor. For through the Law I died to the Law, so that I might live to God. I have been crucified with Christ; and it is no longer I who live, but Christ lives in me; and the life which I now live in the flesh I live by faith in the Son of God, who loved me and gave Himself up for me." (Galatians 2:16-20)

"So Jesus said to them again, 'Truly, truly, I say to you, I am the door of the sheep. All who came before Me are thieves and robbers, but the sheep did not hear them. I am the door; if anyone enters through Me, he will be saved, and will go in and out and find pasture. The thief comes only to steal and kill and destroy; I came that they may have life, and have it abundantly.'" (John 10:7-10)

"But the eleven disciples proceeded to Galilee, to the mountain which Jesus had designated. When they saw Him, they worshiped Him; but some were doubtful. And Jesus came up and spoke to them, saying, 'All authority has been given to Me in heaven and on earth. Go therefore and make disciples of all the nations, baptizing them in the name of the Father and the Son and the Holy Spirit, teaching them to observe all that I commanded you; and lo, I am with you always, even to the end of the age." (Matthew 28:16-20)

You have been changed in many ways. God wants to use you to help others to come to know Him. Are you willing to share the joys and peace that you feel about Jesus Christ? God can use you in your workplace, recreational activities, and with complete strangers. Are you willing to spread the Gospel? Think about some places that you can let your life shine. What will a new person say about you when you meet them? Think about some of the questions and write down your thoughts.

_____

_____

_____

_____

_____

_____

What are some things you would like God to do in your life in a year? In five years?

_____

_____

_____

_____

_____

_____

_____

_____

_____

_____

_____

_____

_____

Chapter 12

Amazing to Be Free and Growing

You have come a long way!!! No matter the struggles that will come, you know God will be with you as long as you are faithful to His Word. Always remember how God saved you, and never become too self-righteous or holy. People are looking for God and need to know about how Jesus Christ died for their sins. Be the light and the example as Jesus was for his disciples and the people of His time. Keep your heart pure and free from judgment or condemnation of others. Always remember, only God has a heaven or hell to place people in.

"Do not judge so that you will not be judged. For in the way you judge, you will be judged; and by your standard of measure, it will be measured to you. Why do you look at the speck that is in your brother's eye, but do not notice the log that is in your own eye? Or how can you say to your brother, 'Let me take the speck out of your eye,' and behold, the log is in your own eye? You hypocrite, first take the log out of your own eye, and then you will see clearly to take the speck out of your brother's eye. Do not give what is holy to dogs, and do not throw your pearls before swine, or they will trample them under their feet, and turn and tear you to pieces. Ask, and it will be given to you; seek, and you will find; knock, and it will be opened to you. For everyone who asks receives, and he who seeks finds, and to him who knocks it will be opened. Or what man is there among you who, when his son asks for a loaf, will give him a stone? Or if he asks for a fish, he will not give him a snake, will he? If you then, being evil, know how to give good gifts to your children, how much more will your Father who is in heaven give what is good to those who ask Him! In everything, therefore, treat people the same way

you want them to treat you, for this is the Law and the Prophets. Enter through the narrow gate; for the gate is wide and the way is broad that leads to destruction, and there are many who enter through it. For the gate is small and the way is narrow that leads to life, and there are few who find it. Beware of the false prophets, who come to you in sheep's clothing, but inwardly are ravenous wolves. You will know them by their fruits. Grapes are not gathered from thorn bushes nor figs from thistles, are they? So every good tree bears good fruit, but the bad tree bears bad fruit. A good tree cannot produce bad fruit, nor can a bad tree produce good fruit. Every tree that does not bear good fruit is cut down and thrown into the fire. So then, you will know them by their fruits. 'Not everyone who says to Me, 'Lord, Lord,' will enter the kingdom of heaven, but he who does the will of My Father who is in heaven will enter. Many will say to Me on that day, 'Lord, Lord, did we not prophesy in Your name, and in Your name cast out demons, and in Your name perform many miracles?' And then I will declare to them, 'I never knew you; DEPART FROM ME, YOU WHO PRACTICE LAWLESSNESS.'" (Matthew 7:1-23)

Where are you in your life?

_____

_____

_____

_____

_____

_____

What are you grateful for?

_____

_____

_____

_____

_____

_____

Are you making progress in your life to get better and do better socially?

_____

_____

_____

_____

_____

_____

No matter the issues you face, don't give up and know that everything will be fine with God. Stand on the Word of God and continue to grow spiritually. Whatever you seek, seek with God, and ask Him for direction in all you do.

A Final Word

You have reached a major milestone in your life! Congratulations!!! You are on your way, and God is going to use you in a mighty way! When you start feeling discouraged, come back to this workbook and look at how much you have grown. Like me, you are and will always be God's "Work in Progress" child until you die. Don't let anyone tell you otherwise. Lift your head and give God a shout of praise! He is worthy to be praised!

Be Blessed,
Shirley Auguste ☺

www.ingramcontent.com/pod-product-compliance
Lightning Source LLC
La Vergne TN
LVHW081328060426
835513LV00012B/1225